OPEN THE DOORS OF YOUR LIFE
—*WORDS OF LIGHT* IN JAPANESE AND ENGLISH—

EDITED BY SEICHO TANIGUCHI

Published by Nippon Kyobunsha Co. Ltd.,
6-44, Akasaka 9-chome, Minato-ku, Tokyo 107-8674.
No part of this publication may be reproduced
in any form or by any means without permission
in writing from the publisher.
Copyright © 2005 by Seicho-No-Ie.
All rights reserved. Printed in Japan.

First Edition 2005
Fifth Edition 2009

ISBN978-4-531-05248-6

人生の扉を開く

日英対訳で読む ひかりの言葉

OPEN THE DOORS OF YOUR LIFE
WORDS OF LIGHT IN JAPANESE AND ENGLISH

谷口清超監修
EDITED BY SEICHO TANIGUCHI

日本教文社

はじめに

　本書は「生長の家」の日めくりカレンダー『ひかりの言葉』の日英対訳版です。生長の家総裁・谷口清超先生が監修を始められた1987～1989年版の3カ年分を一冊にまとめました。この『ひかりの言葉』は主文と脇文とから成り、毎年新たに精選された31日分の真理の言葉が、主文で端的に、脇文でより詳しく説かれています。これまで"英文日訓"として親しまれてきました「英文入りひかりの言葉」では主文のみが英訳されておりましたが、本書の発刊を機に脇文の英訳も新たに加えました。生長の家の教えが日々の指針となり、幸せな人生の扉を開く心の糧となることを願ってやみません。

　　　　　　　　　　　　　　　　　　　　　　日本教文社

Preface

This book is a Japanese-English version of the Seicho-No-Ie calendar *Words of Light*. It is a collection of three years of the calendar (1987 to 1989) beginning with the 1987 calendar when Rev. Seicho Taniguchi, the President of Seicho-No-Ie, first began to edit *Words of Light*. The original calendar is composed of the main text and its explanation. Each year thirty-one new words of Truth are carefully selected. The straightforward words of the main text are then examined in detail in the accompanying explanation. Until now *Words of Light* contained only an English translation of the main text. In this book, however, we have added a new English translation of the explanation. We sincerely pray that the Seicho-No-Ie teachings will become a guide in your daily life and mental sustenance that opens the doors to your happiness.

Nippon Kyobunsha

目　次
CONTENTS

1987 ·················7

1988 ·················71

1989 ·················135

参考図書　References······198

1987

★

ひかりの言葉
WORDS OF LIGHT

毎日があなたにとって元旦である 1

　朝目が覚めたら、その時を一年の元旦のように思うがよろしい。そしてすべての人々に「お目出とう。好（よ）い年が明けまして有りがとうございます」と挨拶し得るほどに"新生の気分"になっていなければならないのである。「自覚の生まれ変わり」である。　（谷口雅春著『聖経版 続 真理の吟唱』より）

Each day is the first day of a new year for you.

When getting up in the morning think that it is the first day of the year. You must have a feeling of rebirth that makes you want to say to everyone "Happy New Year! It's the start of a fine year! Thank you!" It is the *rebirth of our awakening.*

From *Seikyôban Zoku Shinri no Ginshô* (Meditations on Truth II, sutra edition) by Masaharu Taniguchi.

自己の内なる理想を生きよ 2

　もし諸君が、高邁に理想を生き、正義を貫き魂の純粋性を失わなかったならば、内より「汝は勝利者である。偉大なる者である」とよびかけてくれるであろう。真の人間の価値は「彼が何を持つか」ということにはないのであって、「彼が何であるか」ということにあるのである。

（谷口雅春著『青年の書』より）

Live your indwelling ideal.

Friends, if you have not lost the purity of your soul to live nobly your ideal with righteousness, you will hear a voice from within: "You are a winner! You are great!" *The value of the true human being is not the amount of his possessions but his inner essence.*

From *Seinen no Sho* (For Young People) by Masaharu Taniguchi.

「認める」ことによって現われてくる 3

　いかに多くの宝が庫の中に蔵われていようとも灯火がそこになければその宝は無いに等しい。だから諸君よ、諸君の子供にそして諸君の教え子に宿っているところの「神性」（神からの大遺伝）を認めることから始めよ。その「認める力」の輝きによって、いかなる悪癖も悪遺伝も根絶する――。

　　（谷口雅春著『生命の實相』頭注版第14巻より）

Through *recognition* the indwelling Divinity will appear.

No matter how great the treasures kept in the treasure house, if there is no light, the treasures are practically nonexistent. Friends, let us begin by recognizing the indwelling *Divinity* (Great Inheritance from God) in our children and students. Every bad habit and genetic inheritance will be wiped away through the brightness of *our power of recognition.*

From *Seimei no Jissô* (Truth of Life), vol. 14 by Masaharu Taniguchi.

感謝の力は偉大なるかな

　父母に対して感謝する心になると、病気がすばらしくよく治ります。何故かというと、自分を生んでくれ、育ててくれた人への感謝は、「生きていてありがたい、生んでくれて有難い」という気持でありますから、その生み育てられた生命力がよみがえってきて、活発に働きはじめるのです。

　　　　　　　（谷口清超著『病いが消える』より）

How great is the power of gratitude.

Illness heals wonderfully when we acquire the mind of gratitude to our parents. Why? Gratitude to those who bore and raised us is the happiness being born and living in this world. The life power that gave birth to and raised us will be revived and begin to work energetically.

From *Yamai ga Kieru* (Illness Vanishes) by Seicho Taniguchi.

真の裕(ゆた)かさは愛の心にある

5

　意識の世界に於(お)いては物質の豊富よりも、愛念のゆたかさによって、幸福の幅と広さと深さとが変わって来るのである。物質の豊かさによる幸福は儚(はかな)いものであるけれども、愛の豊かさによる幸福は、愛は神より来(きた)り、神は永遠の存在であるから、永遠に消えることはないのである。

（谷口雅春著『聖経版 続 真理の吟唱』より）

True abundance is found in a mind of love.

In the world of consciousness, the width, extent and depth of happiness changes more through an abundance of loving thoughts than material abundance. While the happiness from material abundance is transient, the happiness from abundant love never vanishes eternally because love comes from God and God is an eternal existence.

From *Seikyôban Zoku Shinri no Ginshô* (Meditations on Truth II, sutra edition) by Masaharu Taniguchi.

生命は「生長」するためにある 6

　生命の生長は毎日行なわれるということを知らなければならない。それは毎日生長するのだ。今日発達すべきはずの生長を明日に延ばすならば、生長はそれだけ遅れる。一分一秒でも生命の生長をおくらすことをするな。せっかくきざしている生命のエネルギーを無駄に放散さすな。

　　　　（谷口雅春著『生命の實相』頭注版第14巻より）

Life is for the sake of *growth*.

We must know that the growth of life happens daily. Life grows by the day. If we put off today's life growth until tomorrow, our growth will be delayed to that extent. Do not delay life's growth for even a minute or a second. Do not dissipate the precious energy that life is germinating.

From *Seimei no Jissô* (Truth of Life), vol. 14 by Masaharu Taniguchi.

無我に徹し切るとき奇蹟が起る

　無我のところに神があらわれるとか「無我即神」とかいわれております。報いもとめず献労して病気が治ることがあるのも、報いをもとめない事そのことが「無我」であり、無我のところに神があらわれるからです。——奇蹟的に病気が快癒する例があるのも、同一の原理から来るのです。

　　（谷口雅春著作集第5巻『人間無病の原理』より）

When you are absolutely selfless miracles will happen.

It is said that God appears where there is selflessness and that *selflessness* is *God*. Illness heals when we work devotedly without seeking reward because the act of not seeking reward is *selflessness* and God appears in selflessness. The examples of miraculous recoveries from illness are also the result of this principle.

From *Ningen Mubyô no Genri* (Principle of Perfect Health for Human Beings), Taniguchi Masaharu Chosakushû, vol. 5.

神はまさに今あなたの中にある

　常に今を生かして、全力を出し切ろう。それはあせることではない。アクセクと我(が)の努力をするのでもない。神に全托し、神のいのちを、ひたすら生き切る。祈りに徹し、愛行(あいぎょう)に徹して、いのちを今の一点に集中する。そのとき、神があなたを通して、悠々(ゆうゆう)と働き給うのである。

　　　　（谷口清超著『さわやかに生きよう』より）

Beyond doubt, at this very moment, God dwells within you.

Always make best use of the present moment and do your very best. I do not mean to *make undue haste* and work busily through the power of your ego. It means to entrust everything to God and completely live the life of God. It means to wholeheartedly pray and perform deeds of love and focus your *life* solely on your present goal. At that moment God will work quietly through you.

From *Sawayakani Ikiyô* (Let's Live a Refreshing Life) by Seicho Taniguchi.

親が心に描くことが子供に現われてくる

「うちの子はよく出来るすばらしい子だ」と信じたり、現状を肯定していると、その通りすばらしくやってくれますが、「うちの子は懶け癖(なまぐせ)がついて困る」などと思っていると、その通り益々懶けて勉強しなくなる。だから「すばらしい子だ、深切で明るく素直なよい子だ」と信じてあげればよいのです。　　　　（谷口清超著『父と母のために』より）

What parents conceive in their minds will be manifest in their children.

When we believe "My child is a wonderful child who does well in everything," and affirm his circumstances in this way, our children will be as wonderful as we believed them to be. But when we think such thoughts as "My child has lazy habits," he will in fact become increasingly lazy and neglect his studies. That is why it is best to believe: "My child is a wonderful child! He is a kind, cheerful and a good, honest child!"

From *Chichi to Haha no Tame ni* (For Fathers and Mothers) by Seicho Taniguchi.

自分の仕事を讃美し
いつも感謝して暮そう

　讃美の言葉と感情とが、神の世界にある"実相無限の富"に波長が合い、それが具象化して"現実の富"となってあらわれる契機をつくることになるのである。自分の職業を讃美し、自分の事業に感謝することにしたら、その事業が発展し、素晴しい収入が得られるようになった実例もある。

　　　　（谷口雅春著『新版　栄える生活365章』より）

Live your life by praising your work and always being grateful.

Words and feelings of praise create an opportunity to tune our wavelengths to the *Infinite Wealth of the True Image* in God's World and externalize it as *actual wealth*. There are examples of businesses growing and receiving a wonderful income from praising one's occupation and being grateful to one's business.

From *Shinpan Sakaeru Seikatsu 365 Shô* (365 Keys to a Prosperous Life, new ed.) by Masaharu Taniguchi.

親に感謝する心は「いのち」の根を培う

　皆さんを小さい時から、心から愛し育てて下さった父母がおられた。そんな「有難い」ところを、もっともっと強く心に思いうかべ、恵まれた自分であったことに感謝し、コトバに出して言ったりすると、「生きがい」が出て来、「生きているよろこび」がわき、生命力がモリモリと噴出するのである。　　　　（谷口清超著『人は天窓から入る』より）

Being grateful to our parents cultivates the root of *life*.

You have a father and mother who loved you from the bottom of their hearts and raised you from an early age. When we increasingly call to mind the *blessings* from our parents, are grateful to those blessings and express them in words, we will feel the *worth of living* and the *joy of being born in this world* and life power will well forth vigorously from us.

From *Hito wa Tenmado Kara Hairu* (We Enter From Heaven's Window) by Seicho Taniguchi.

明るく努力すれば必ず道が開ける

12

　行動の結果がハッキリとあらわれてくるには、ある時間的ズレがある。生活を光の方向にふりむけ、善意をもって生きはじめるならば、その結果が、いつか必ずあらわれてくる。必ず、ある時間たって、あらわれる。このことを信じ、安心し、善行をなせ、愛行せよ。

　　　　　（谷口清超著『輝く日々のために』より）

If we keep striving cheerfully, the way will not fail to open.

It takes time for the results of our efforts to appear clearly. When we turn our lives to the light and start to live with good intentions, results are certain to appear some day. They will surely appear after the passage of time. Believe this truth and engage in good deeds and acts of love with peace of mind.

From *Kagayaku Hibi no Tame ni* (For a Shining Daily Life) by Seicho Taniguchi.

13 子供は夫々(それぞれ)尊い個性を持っている

　子供をよくしようと思う時に、大人の、しかも自分だけの尺度でもって判断しすぎて善意を評価するといけないのであります。人間というものは皆(みな)個性がちがう。個性がちがうところにそこに価値がある。桜は桜でその良さを認め、バラはバラでその良さを認めなければならないのであります。　（谷口雅春著『生命の實相』頭注版第14巻より）

Each child possesses his own precious personality.

When you try to improve a child it is wrong to judge his good intentions by using the yardstick of adults excessively, which is, in addition, *their own measure.* The personalities of human beings differ. There is value in that difference. We must recognize the good qualities of a cherry blossom as a cherry blossom and of the rose as a rose.

From *Seimei no Jissô* (Truth of Life), vol. 14 by Masaharu Taniguchi.

原因はすべて自分の心にある

　人間は、心によって自分の運命をつくり出す。周囲が悪いからこんなになったと、人はよく考え勝ちであるが、それでは自分自身の自主性など何処(どこ)にもないであろう。不足の心は不足の環境を生み出す。この不平不満の心を、感謝の心に変え、"与える心"になると一切がよくなる。
（谷口清超ヒューマン・ブックス9『善意の世界』より）

The cause lies totally within your mind.

Human beings create their destiny through their minds. While people are prone to think that their surroundings are to blame, by so doing they ignore their independence. A mind concentrated on what is lacking gives rise to surroundings of insufficiency. Everything will improve when we change our discontented and complaining mind to the *mind that gives.*

From *Zen-i no Sekai* (World of Good Intentions), Taniguchi Seicho Human Books, vol. 9.

陽気を失うとき生長はとまる

　明るい人間でないとだめ。どんな才能を持っていても、明るさがないとのびて行かない。いのちは光に向ってのびる。それは、一粒の種子(たね)が光に向ってのびて行くようなものだ。明るくあれ。心に深切(しんせつ)な思いをもて。何事にも善意を見出せ。人々の、神の万物のあたたかい「愛」を味わうことが大切である。

　　　　　（谷口清超著『輝く日々のために』より）

Growth stops when we lose our cheerfulness.

We must be bright and cheerful. No matter what talents we possess we cannot grow without cheerfulness. *Life* grows by facing the light. It is like a seed that grows toward the sunlight. Be bright and cheerful. Fill your heart with kindness. Discover good intentions in all things. It is important to savor the warm *love* of people and God's creation.

From *Kagayaku Hibi no Tame ni* (For a Shining Daily Life) by Seicho Taniguchi.

16
神様は出来ない問題を与え給わない

　問題から逃げ出そうとすることなく、問題を静かな心になってよく見詰め、よく精査せよ。必ず解決の緒(いとぐち)が見出されるのである。四方がふさがっていても、必ず上方はあいているのである。上方は"神の道"である。神に向えば、あらゆる問題は解決の道を見出し得るのである。

（谷口雅春著『若人のための78章』より）

God does not assign unsolvable problems.

Do not attempt to run away from a problem. Look hard at it while in a peaceful state of mind and carefully examine it. You will surely find the clue to solve it. Even if every corner is blocked, the way above is always open. The way above is *God's path*. The way to solve all problems will be found by turning to God.

From *Wakôdo no Tame no 78 Shô* (Seventy-Eight Lessons for Young People) by Masaharu Taniguchi.

愛のことばが最高の贈り物である 17

　愛のこもった深切な言葉は、相手に対して強壮剤として働くのである。愛語を語ることを惜しんではならない。しかし愛のないただの挨拶にすぎない形式だけの愛語はニセモノであり、虚栄であり綺語(きご)である。本当に美点を見る気持になれば、心からウソでない賞讃の言葉が湧き出て来るものである。（谷口雅春著『新版　女性の幸福365章』より）

Words of love are the greatest gift.

Kind words that are filled with love work on others like a tonic. You must not refrain from speaking loving words. However, formal expressions that are empty of love are falsehoods, vanities and only flowery language. If we truly wish to see another's good points, genuine words of praise will well up from the bottom of our hearts.

From *Shinpan Josei no Kôfuku 365 Shô* (365 Keys to Women's Happiness, new ed.) by Masaharu Taniguchi.

18
神にまかせよ
自然にその時が来る

　凡(あら)ゆる問題解決には、適当な時期というものがある。──「ある時期」が来て、はじめて芽が生(は)え、花が開く。その時期が来るまでは、内部の力をたくわえることに専心するがよい。あわてるな。人生は永(なが)い。あなたの人生が「永遠」であることを、決して忘れてはならないのである。

　　　　　（谷口清超著『輝く日々のために』より）

Trust in God.
The time will come of itself.

There is the appropriate time to solve any problem. When a *certain time* comes, for the first time will shoots appear, grow and bloom. Until that time arrives, it is best to devote ourselves to storing our inner power. Do not rush! Life is long. You must never forget that your life is *eternal.*

From *Kagayaku Hibi no Tame ni* (For a Shining Daily Life) by Seicho Taniguchi.

些細（ささい）なことが重大である

19

　アメリカのすぐれた大会社の女性秘書は、心をこめて来客にコーヒーを入れてくれるという。それが、重役達の仕事に大いに役立っている。つまらぬような仕草が、実はそうではない。やさしいコトバ、ちょっとした挨拶、そんな所から会社やその団体の体質が判断され、信用がつき仕事が拡大するのだ。

　　　　　　（谷口清超著『輝く日々のために』より）

The small things are of great importance.

A secretary in a large and fine American company wholeheartedly serves coffee to visitors. Her efforts greatly help the work of the company's directors. Seemingly worthless actions are actually by no means so. Kind words and a simple greeting determine the nature of a company or organization, build its trust and expand its business.

From *Kagayaku Hibi no Tame ni* (For a Shining Daily Life) by Seicho Taniguchi.

"愛"は敵を味方にする 20

　「北風と太陽」の話があるだろう。——太陽が北風に代って温かく照りはじめると、旅人は自然にマントをぬいで、汗をぬぐったという。北風は「力」のあらわれであり「太陽」は愛の象徴だ。愛はいかなる暴力よりも強いし、いかなる権力よりもたのみがいがある。愛の生活をしよう。

　　　　　　　（谷口清超著『輝く日々のために』より）

Love turns an adversary into a friend.

You have probably heard the story of the North Wind and the Sun. When the Sun took the place of the North Wind and shined, the travelers naturally removed their capes and wiped away their sweat. The North Wind is an expression of *power* and the Sun is a symbol of *love*. Love is stronger than any force and more dependable than any authority. Let us live a life of love.

From *Kagayaku Hibi no Tame ni* (For a Shining Daily Life) by Seicho Taniguchi.

断言は大いなる力である

　もっと積極的な、肯定的断定法によって、正しい人間生活を堂々と歩むところの自己を断言しなければならない。既にそのような自分であるのだと宣言し、その断定的コトバを日毎夜毎くりかえし唱えるようにするならば、必ずや真実の自己があらわれ出るに違いないのである。

　　　　　　（谷口清超著『人は天窓から入る』より）

Positive affirmation is great power.

We must positively affirm our self which magnificently walks the proper path of life by using a more positive and affirmative conclusive method. If we declare that we are already that self and repeat those conclusive words both morning and night, our true self will appear without fail.

From *Hito wa Tenmado Kara Hairu* (We Enter From Heaven's Window) by Seicho Taniguchi.

正しい祈りはあなたを美しくする

22

　祈りを籠^こめた眼は、深くたたえた淵^{ふち}のような深遠さをもっている。顔貌^{がんぼう}に深さと崇高な美しさを加えようと思うならば、常に祈ることである。祈りによって神に心を馳^はせている顔貌ほど気尚^{けだか}く美しきものはない。それが度々繰返されるとき、深い美しさを底から湛^{たた}え得るようになるのである。

（谷口雅春著『新版　女性の幸福365章』より）

Correct prayer will beautify your life.

Eyes that are immersed in prayer have the profundity of a deep pool. If you seek to add depth and sublime beauty to your countenance you must engage in constant prayer. There is no more dignified beauty than the countenance of hastening toward God through prayer. Through repeated prayer a profound beauty fills us from the bottom of our soul.

From *Shinpan Josei no Kôfuku 365 Shô* (365 Keys to Women's Happiness, new ed.) by Masaharu Taniguchi.

23 ほめるとき埋蔵された力が出てくる

　大人は、子供の学業や仕事に対して大いに喜んでやるのがよいのである。「生長の家」では信と愛と讃嘆との三つを実際生活上最も必要な徳であるとするのである。信と愛とは「心の徳」だ。讃嘆は「心の徳」を外にあらわして現実的の力とする言葉の力であるのである。

　　　　（谷口雅春著『生命の實相』頭注版第14巻より）

When praised hidden power comes forth.

Adults should take great delight in children's studies and work. *Seicho-No-Ie* believes that faith, love and praise are the most essential virtues in actual life. Faith and love are *mental virtues.* Praise is the power of the word that manifests the *mental virtues* in the outside word as actual power.

From *Seimei no Jissô* (Truth of Life), vol. 14 by Masaharu Taniguchi.

24 心が病いをつくり そして病いを癒す

　今迄の心配や不安や、争いや憎しみの心から、安らかな、調和した、感謝の心に変らなければ、肉体の治癒は行われ難いのである。肉体の場合は、心が自動的に肉体を変化させる仕組みになっているから、心が真に大安心し、調和し、感謝にみたされて来れば自動的に治癒されて、健康になってゆく。　　　（谷口清超著『人は天窓から入る』より）

The mind creates and also heals disease.

Unless you change your mind from worry, anxiety, discord and hatred to peace, harmony and gratitude, it is difficult to heal the physical body. Since the body is arranged so that the mind automatically brings change to it, when the mind is truly at peace, in a state of harmony and filled with gratitude the body automatically heals and recovers its health.

From *Hito wa Tenmado Kara Hairu* (We Enter From Heaven's Window) by Seicho Taniguchi.

神からの賜は無数にある

　愛する妻子がいる。住む家がある。どんな小さな茅屋であろうとも、もともと素裸の我が身にとっては、何という有難い賜物であろう。夫も妻も、又兄弟も、私達をこよなく愛して下さる。万金を積んでも動かすことの出来ぬ愛が、私達をびっしりと、取り囲んでいて離れない。

　　　　（谷口清超著『さわやかに生きよう』より）

God's gifts are countless.

There is our loving wife and children. There is also our home. No matter how humble our home, for our self that is free of ego and attachment these are indescribably wonderful gifts. Our spouse or siblings love us without end. Love that cannot be moved by all the money in the world thoroughly surrounds us forever.

From *Sawayakani Ikiyô* (Let's Live a Refreshing Life) by Seicho Taniguchi.

26 "愛"は美しい花びらのように人生を飾る

　乱れ咲く花には取越苦労もなければ気がねも見得もない。素直にせい一杯の喜びをぶちまけて、大地を美しく飾る。そこには健康な空気がみなぎっている。親子、夫婦、兄弟が、正しい位置に於いて精一杯愛し合える世界がそこにある。それは太陽の直射する明るい輝かしい世界だ。

　　　　（谷口清超新書文集2『神は生きている』より）

Like beautiful flower petals, *love* adds beauty to human life.

In the flowers that bloom randomly there is no sign of needless worry, *constraint* or *ostentation*. They honestly and obediently express their joy with all their might and beautifully adorn the earth. An air of health overflows about them. And there we find the world where parents and children, spouses and siblings love one another to the utmost according to their proper place. It is the bright and shining world under the direct rays of the sun.

From *Kami wa Ikiteiru* (God Is Alive), Taniguchi Seicho Shinshobunshû, vol. 2.

親は子供の心に種子(たね)を蒔(ま)く

27

　われらは子供の心に、美しい花を開き、美味しい果実(み)を結ぶような種子を蒔いておこうではないか。平和の種子、健康の種子、和合の種子、寛大の種子、自信の種子、深切の種子をこそ子供の時に蒔こうではないか。日常生活の子供の前で言葉や行為で実行して見せるに限るのである。

（谷口雅春著『生命の實相』頭注版第14巻より）

Parents sow the seeds of their children's thoughts.

Should we not sow in our children's mind seeds that bring forth beautiful flowers and delicious fruit? Should we not indeed sow seeds of peace, health, harmony, generosity, confidence and kindness in them from an early age? The best way of doing so is the example of our daily words and deeds in the presence of our children.

From *Seimei no Jissô* (Truth of Life), vol. 14 by Masaharu Taniguchi.

あなたの中に「無限」がある 28

　やったことのない事をやるには、ある種の勇気がいる。堂々として未知の原野を踏破せよ。「やったことがないからできない」などと弱音を吐くな。やればできる。あなたは「神の子」だ、無限力だ。無限の可能性が噴出しようとして、あなたの中にうごめいていることを知れ。

　　　　（谷口清超著『輝く日々のために』より）

There is *infinite* within you.

Courage is needed to do something new. Let us grandly hike to an unknown wilderness. Do not complain that it is impossible because you have never done so. You can if you try. You are a *child of God*! You are infinite power! Know that infinite possibility is bubbling within you and about to gush forth.

From *Kagayaku Hibi no Tame ni* (For a Shining Daily Life) by Seicho Taniguchi.

正しい信仰は全ての人に安らぎを与える 29

　信仰とは決して神秘な、曖昧(あいまい)な、定めがたき感情もしくは情緒ではないのである。各人の、美しき、朗(ほが)かな、純な、愛深き魂にやどりて、今活(い)きていますところの「神の子」の存在を信ずる信仰である。正しき信仰とは人の魂に安心を与えるものでなければならない。

　　　　　　　（谷口雅春著『若人のための78章』より）

Proper religious faith imparts peace of mind to all.

Faith is never mysterious, vague and uncertain feelings or emotions. It dwells in the beautiful, serene, pure and deeply loving soul and the faith that believes in the existence of the *child of God* that is alive at this very moment. Proper faith always brings peace to the soul.

From *Wakôdo no Tame no 78 Shô* (Seventy-Eight Lessons for Young People) by Masaharu Taniguchi.

感謝と確信と明るい言葉が平和を実現する 30

　イエスは「神よ、あなたは常に私の祈りに応(こた)え給いし事を感謝いたします」と先ず"感謝"の言葉を述べて神に対したのである。そして、祈りの実現に確信をもってから、その確信をもって自分の願望の実現を言葉の力をもって宣言したのである。その方法によってラザロは癒やされたのである。
　　　　　　　　（谷口雅春著『聖経版 続 真理の吟唱』より）

Gratitude, conviction and bright words will realize peace.

Jesus first thanked God that his prayers were always answered, and with that conviction he declared the realization of his wishes through the power of the word. This is how Jesus brought Lazarus back to life.

From *Seikyôban Zoku Shinri no Ginshô* (Meditations on Truth II, sutra edition) by Masaharu Taniguchi.

31 要らぬものを掴むな
要るものが入って来ない

　不平が起るのは、心が一つの物に凝り過ぎて他の恵みを見る余裕がないからである。悩みは心にあるのであって物にあるのではない。凝りを放下して、眼を他に一転せよ。どんなに吾らは多くの恵みに取捲かれていることだろう。掴みを放す事、心の中が空手になる事が万事の秘訣である。

　　　　　（谷口雅春著『新版　ひかりの語録』より）

Do not grasp the unnecessary. The essentials will not come to you.

Complaints are the result of our inability to see other blessings because our mind is overly preoccupied with a single object or thing. Our suffering exists in our mind and not the object or thing itself. Discard your *preoccupations* and completely change your point of view. How great are the blessings that surround us. The secret of all things in life is to release our grasp and empty our mind of its attachments.

From *Shinpan Hikari no Goroku* (Sayings of Light, new ed.) by Masaharu Taniguchi.

1988

★

ひかりの言葉
WORDS OF LIGHT

1 今こそが新生のための
チャンスである

　もし過去の生活で思わしくないことがあったら、この際(さい)一新してしまうがよい。そのためには勇気が必要だ。その勇気は、あなたの中にちゃんとそなわっている。思い切って神を信じ、神に全托し、神の大海に飛び込むと、ブクブク沈むと思いきや、ポッカリと浮いて、楽ちんこの上なしということになる。　　　（谷口清超著『輝く人生のために』より）

Now is indeed the chance for rebirth.

Although you may have had unpleasant experiences in the past, renew yourself now. Courage is needed for this, and that courage is perfectly prepared within you. Resolutely believe in God, trust in Him and dive into His Great Ocean. When you do so you will not sink but float and there is nothing more pleasant than this.

From *Kagayaku Jinsei no Tame ni* (For a Shining Human Life) by Seicho Taniguchi.

切なる願いはかならずかなえられる 2

　希望は実現の母である。あなたの心の底深く催(もよお)して来るところの願いは、既(すで)に実相に於(おい)て成就しているのである。これを「みこころが既に天に成る」というのである。私たちが切にその実現を心に念じ、波長を合わすようにつとめる時、必ずそれは成就するのである、自信をもってよい。信じて祈れ。

　　　　（谷口雅春著『新版　生活の智慧365章』より）

An earnest desire will surely be answered.

Hope is the mother of realization. The desires that come from the depths of your heart are already fulfilled in the True-Image World. This is why Jesus prayed that his Father's will was already realized in Heaven. When we earnestly pray for the realization of our desires and strive to attune our mental wavelengths to them, they will certainly be realized. Have confidence! Have confidence and pray!

From *Shinpan Seikatsu no Chie 365 Shô* (365 Keys to Daily Wisdom, new ed.) by Masaharu Taniguchi.

凡ゆる立場での主人公となれ 3

　吾々は内部にある何ものかのために「人生劇場」で熱演を続けているのであります。それは、「随処作主（ずいしょさしゅ）」——凡ゆる立場で主人公となって環境を支配し、大調和を演ずるためです。「主婦」となれば最も美しい優しい「主婦」を演じ、「百姓」になれば世界第一の「百姓」を演ずることです。
（谷口清超ヒューマン・ブックス１『愛と祈りを実現するには』より）

In every respect, become the leading character in the theater of life.

We continue to perform enthusiastically on the *theater of human life* for a certain existence within us. Ours is a *performance of everyday affairs.* We become the leading character of all aspects of our life, rule our surroundings and perform the role of grand harmony. If our role is a *wife* we are the most beautiful and kind *wife.* If our role is a *farmer* we become the world's best *farmer.*

From *Ai to Inori o Jitsugensuru ni wa* (To Realize Love and Prayer), Taniguchi Seicho Human Books, vol. 1.

4

一切萬事吾より出でて吾に還る
ばんじ　われ

　悟りというものは、一切を外的原因だとして、責任を外に負わしていた者が、一転一切の責任は自己にありと、脚下照顧、自己に反照して、一切萬事吾より出でて吾に還ると知ることである。外に神を求めていた迷信から一転して、功徳の本源は自己にありと自覚する事が真の宗教であるのである。　　（新選谷口雅春選集11『叡智の斷片』より）

All things come forth from and return to oneself.

Enlightenment is the realization that all the outward causes and responsibilities for our troubles are of our own making. It is to reflect upon ourselves and know that everything comes forth and returns to us. We turn from the superstitious belief that seeks God outside ourselves and realize that the source of all virtues is within us. This is true religion.

From *Eichi no Danpen* (Short Pieces of Wisdom), Shinsen Taniguchi Masaharu Senshû, vol. 11.

自己の内なる力が全てを癒す

　自分自身の「生きる力」こそ、自分にとって一等の名医であります。なぜなら、自然療能という医師は、自分の内にチャンといる名医だから、いかなる医師よりも、迅速(じんそく)に処置がとれ、内にいて患部の状態を知りつくしているから、その処置をまちがえるということは決してないのであります。
　　　　　（谷口雅春著『生命の實相』頭注版第2巻より）

One's indwelling power will heal all.

Our *power to live* is indeed the finest doctor for us. Why? The doctor called Natural Healing Ability perfectly resides within us. He therefore treats us faster than any doctor and he knows our condition thoroughly. For that reason he never administers the wrong treatment.

From *Seimei no Jissô* (Truth of Life), vol. 2 by Masaharu Taniguchi.

人は仕事を通して神の愛を伝える

　会社の仕事でも、個人の仕事でも、どれだけ多くの人々をよろこばせ、幸せにしてあげ、奉仕することが出来るかということを考えなくてはなりません。この「与え合い」の明るい信仰が凡(すべ)ての人々に行きわたるとき、本当の日本があらわれ、世界のすべての人々に貢献できる「神の国」となりうるのです。

　　　　　（谷口清超著『栄える人々のために』より）

Through our work we convey God's love.

Our goal must be to bring joy and happiness and serve as many people as possible through our company or private work. When this cheerful faith of *giving to one another* is conveyed to all people, the true Japan will appear and become the *Kingdom of God* that contributes to the people of the world.

From *Sakaeru Hitobito no Tame ni* (For Prosperous People) by Seicho Taniguchi.

7 「ねばならぬ」を捨てよ 真の自由が得られる

　こうでなければならぬ、ああでなければならぬというのは人間の小智才覚の凝りであります。この「心で掴んでいる凝り」をパッと放してしまうと、人間は本来の自由を得る——どうしなくとも生きられる本来の自由な自分自身を見いだすのです。ここに人間生命を生かす奥義があるのです。

　　　　（谷口雅春著『生命の實相』頭注版第5巻より）

Throw away the *idea of must* and you will acquire true freedom.

The thinking that things must be a certain way is the preoccupation of human shallow wisdom and wit. When we *release* these *preoccupations suddenly we acquire true freedom*. We will discover our original free Self that cannot help but live with freedom. Here is the secret to enliven human life.

From *Seimei no Jissô* (Truth of Life), vol. 5 by Masaharu Taniguchi.

8 困難や不幸は
我(が)の崩れゆく過程である

　真の人間には死はないのであって、偽物の人間、即(すなわ)ち偽我(ぎが)にのみ死があるのです。偽物の我(われ)が死に切った時、真の吾(われ)があらわれるのであります。困難や不幸は、偽物の我(が)の崩れゆく過程ですから、困難は無いのであり、喜びのみ独(ひと)り在(あ)るのです。人生には喜びのみが充満しているのです。
（谷口清超ヒューマン・ブックス１『愛と祈りを実現するには』より）

郵便はがき

料金受取人払郵便

赤坂支店
承認
9013

差出有効期間
2022年4月
30日まで

1 0 7 - 8 7 8 0

2 3 5

東京都港区赤坂
　　　　9-6-44

日本教文社

　　　愛読者カード係行

|ıl|ı|·ıı·|ıl|ıl|ıı||ı|ı·|ı|ı·|ı|ı·|ı|ı·|ı|ı·|ı|ı·|ı|ı·|ı|ıı|

ご購読ありがとうございます。本欄は、新刊やおすすめ情報等の
ご案内の資料とさせていただきます。ご記入の上、投函下さい。

(フリガナ)

お名前　　　　　　　　　　　　　　　　　　　　　男・女／年齢　　歳

ご住所　〒

　　　都道　　　　　　　市区
　　　府県　　　　　　　町村

電話　　（　　　）　　　　　e-mail　　　＠

ご職業　　　　　　　　　　　ご購読新聞・雑誌名

よく使うインターネットサービス名

下記の小社刊の月刊誌を購読されていますか。
□いのちの環　□白鳩　□日時計24
（見本誌のご希望　□いのちの環　□白鳩　□日時計24）

・新刊案内　□希望する　　・おすすめ情報の案内　□希望する
・図書目録　□希望する　　・メルマガ(無料)　　　□希望する

愛読者カード

今後の参考にさせていただきます。本書のご感想・ご意見をお寄せ下さい。

◇今回ご購入された図書名

◇ご購入の動機
1. 書店で見て　　　　　　　　5. 新聞広告を見て(紙名　　　　　　　　)
2. インターネットやケータイサイトで　6. 人に勧められて
3. 小社の案内を見て　　　　　7. プレゼントされた
4. 小社の月刊誌を見て　　　　8. その他(　　　　　　　　　　　　)

◇ご感想・ご意見

＊いただいたご感想を小社ホームページ等に掲載してもよろしいですか?
□はい　□匿名またはペンネームならよい(　　　　　　)　□いいえ

◇今後お読みになりたいと思う本の企画(内容)や作者

◇小社愛読者カードをお送り下さるのは今回が初めてですか。
　　　　　　　　　　　□はい　□いいえ(　　回め)

◆ご注文カード◆

書　名	著者名	定価	冊数

＊ご注文は電話、FAX、e-mail、ホームページでも承っております。
＊国内送料:一件2000円(税込)以上=送料無料、2000円(税込)未満=送料210円

◇ご記入いただいた個人情報は、小社出版物の企画の参考とさせていただくとともに、ご注文いただいた商品の発送、お支払い確認等の連絡および新刊などの案内をお送りするために利用し、その目的以外での利用はいたしません。

日本教文社
TEL03-3401-9112　FAX03-3401-9139
http://www.kyobunsha.jp

＊アンケートはPCやケータイ、スマートフォンからも送ることが可能です。

Troubles and misfortune are the process of egotism's collapse.

There is no death for the True Human Being. There is death for only the counterfeit self, namely, the false self. When the false self is totally dead, our True Self will appear. Troubles and misfortune are the process of the collapse of our false self. That is why troubles are nonexistent and only joy exists. Human life is overflowing with joy alone.

From *Ai to Inori o Jitsugensuru ni wa* (To Realize Love and Prayer), Taniguchi Seicho Human Books, vol. 1.

困難は必ず解決策を連れて来る

癌とか、癌の疑いなどと言われると、もう死神に追いつめられている土壇場のような気持になる人もいますが、決してそんなものではありません。困難が来たら、必ずよりすばらしい解決策も共につれて来ているのだと思って下さい。しかもそれを解決することによって魂が一層高まって行くのです。　　　　（谷口清超著『病いが消える』より）

Trouble surely brings its own means for a solution.

There are people who think that they are at the point of no return and being pursued by the god of death when they are diagnosed with cancer or it is suspected. Yet that could never be true. When trouble arrives, think that it surely comes with a wonderful solution. And by solving that trouble your soul is far more elevated.

From *Yamai ga Kieru* (Illness Vanishes) by Seicho Taniguchi.

神は積極性を愛し給う 10

　どこまでも積極的であれ。言われたことだけひかえ目にやっているのでは、いつまでたっても実力が出ない。一を言われたら、十をやれ。十を求められたら、どうして二十をやらないか。いのちを出しおしみしてはならぬ。いのちをかけ、首をかけ、名誉も地位も投げ出してやらねば、本当の仕事はできない。

　　　　　　（谷口清超著『輝く日々のために』より）

God loves positive attitudes and efforts.

Be positive in every way! If you do nothing but correct the shortcomings that are pointed out to you, you will never acquire real ability. When one shortcoming is pointed out, make ten corrections. And when you are asked to do ten, why do you hesitate from doing twenty? You must not give of your life grudgingly. Unless you stake your life, position, honor and status, you cannot do real work.

From *Kagayaku Hibi no Tame ni* (For a Shining Daily Life) by Seicho Taniguchi.

夫婦の感謝が教育の根本である

　夫婦が仲良く暮すことは、人間と生れての最大の喜びです。夫婦の心がピッタリして心から感謝し合うようになると、子供は人格の面でも、成績の面でも、健康の面でも不思議なくらいよくなるものです。これは子供と父母とは、身体は別々であっても、心が一つにつながっているからです。

　　　　　（谷口清超著『家庭をたのしく』より）

Gratitude between husband and wife is the foundation of their children's education.

For a husband and wife to live their lives in perfect harmony is the greatest joy of human life. When their minds are joined in oneness and they are grateful to one another from the bottom of their hearts, their children will experience nearly miraculous improvement in even their character, school work and health. This is because the minds of children and their parents are joined in oneness although their bodies are separate from one another.

From *Katei o Tanoshiku* (A Happy Home Life) by Seicho Taniguchi.

12 天地のすべてのものは如来の現成である

　釈迦がお悟りになったとき、「山川草木国土悉皆成仏」とお知りになったのです。今まで物質だと見えていた山も川も、草も木も、国土も、悉く皆物質ではないのであって、現成せる仏のいのちだと悟られたのです。何物も生かさずに措かないところの仏の力が、神の力が吾々を包んでいて下さるのです。

　　（谷口雅春著『新版　希望を叶える365章』より）

Everything in the universe is the perfect manifestation of the Buddha.

When Shakyamuni achieved enlightenment he realized that the mountains, rivers, plants and earth were the Buddha. He awakened to the truth that the mountains, rivers, plants and earth, which seemed until then to be matter, were not matter but the manifestation of the Buddha's life. The power of the Buddha, which cannot help but give life to all things, and the power of God are embracing us.

From *Shinpan Kibô o Kanaeru 365 Shô* (365 Keys to Realize Your Hopes, new ed.) by Masaharu Taniguchi.

人間に最も大切なのは
人を知ることである

　人間と生まれてその人が偉大なる理想をどの広さまで実現し得るか否かということは、その人の自覚が人間そのものを如何なる広さにまで、如何なる深さにまで拡大深化して自覚し得ているかに関っているのである。その発見の度合いにしたがって諸君の生活が一変三変千変万化するのである。
（谷口雅春著『人間そのものの発見とその自覚』より）

The most important thing for human beings is to know themselves.

The extent to which a person realizes his great ideal from being born as a human being depends on the degree to which his awareness expands and deepens about the nature of human beings themselves. Depending on the degree of your realization your life will completely change, once, three times, or an innumerable number of times.

From *Ningen Sonomono no Hakken to Sono Jikaku* (The Discovery and Understanding of Human Beings Themselves) by Masaharu Taniguchi.

柔かく温かく清く美わしい雰囲気が凡てのよきものを作り出す

　広い、のびやかな、豊かな心の持主、その人の傍らにゆけば、愛の雰囲気がほのぼのとただよっていて何ともいえない和やかな気持になれる人——そういう人が本当に心の健康な人であると言う事が出来るのです。その雰囲気から凡ゆるよきもの、幸福なるものが生み出されて来るのです。
（谷口清超ヒューマン・ブックス1『愛と祈りを実現するには』より）

A gentle, warm, pure and beautiful atmosphere brings forth all good things.

The possessor of a broad, unfettered and abundant mind with a warm atmosphere of love that brings an indescribable feeling of peace to those around him—we can say such a person is truly a mentally healthy person. All good and happy things are born from his atmosphere.

From *Ai to Inori o Jitsugensuru ni wa* (To Realize Love and Prayer), Taniguchi Seicho Human Books, vol. 1.

心の眼(まなこ)を開け　全てが見えてくる　15

　健康な心の持主は、たとい自分を悪口(あっこう)し、さばき、罵(のの)しる声が聞こえて来ましょうとも、それを完全に否定してしまうのです。五感六感の方を信ずるのではなく、何も見えない神様を無条件で信ずるのが信仰です。信じ切った時、神様の世界が顕(あらわ)れるのです。眼を開いたとき光が見えるように。
（谷口清超ヒューマン・ブックス１『愛と祈りを実現するには』より）

Open your mind's eye and everything can be seen.

Even when he hears the insults, accusations and abusive language of others, the possessor of a healthy mind completely denies them. Faith is not to believe in the five or the six senses but to unconditionally believe in the unseen God. When we completely believe in God, His World will unfold for us, like seeing the light when we open our eyes.

From *Ai to Inori o Jitsugensuru ni wa* (To Realize Love and Prayer), Taniguchi Seicho Human Books, vol. 1.

16 病気無し悪無しが真実である

　神は善であるから、善のほかのものは造らない。だから悪は存在しないのである。病気は悪であるから存在しない。災難は悪であるから存在しない。存在しないものは無いのである。無いものは如何(いか)に「ある」かの如く見えても無いのである。無いものを「有る」と感じているのは頭脳智(ずのうち)の嘘に過ぎない。

（谷口雅春著『新版　希望を叶える365章』より）

The nonexistence of disease and evil is a fact.

Since God is good, He creates nothing but the good. That is why evil is nonexistent. Since illness is evil, illness does not exist. Since misfortune is evil, misfortune does not exist. What does not exist is nonexistent. No matter how the nonexistent may seem to *exist*, it is nonexistent. To think that the nonexistent *exists* is no more than the gossip of the brain's intelligence.

From *Shinpan Kibô o Kanaeru 365 Shô* (365 Keys to Realize Your Hopes, new ed.) by Masaharu Taniguchi.

17 価値が創造されると真の富が現れる

　本当に「機会」をつかむ人は、職業がないときに、それこそ好機会であると思い、職業があっては出来ないような価値創造をするのであります。価値が創造せられる処(ところ)にのみ本当の富があり、本当の発展があり、本当の再建があり、みずからを助ける者をのみ、神は彼を助け給うのであります。
　（谷口雅春著『若人のための78章』より）

When we create value true wealth appears.

If unemployed, a person who has truly grasped *opportunity* will think of his circumstances as being indeed a good chance and create value that can never be produced through an ordinary job. Only where value is created does true wealth appear, true growth occurs and true rebuilding will is realized. God helps only those who help themselves.

From *Wakôdo no Tame no 78 Shô* (Seventy-Eight Lessons for Young People) by Masaharu Taniguchi.

18 悲しい時ほど大いに笑い笑いぬけ

　高らかな朗らかな笑いは、自然が与えた最良の強壮剤（こうしょう）である。哄笑を爆発さすとき、憂鬱（ゆううつ）な心で抑えつけられていた生理作用はたちまち活発に活動をはじめる。血液の循環は順調になり、自然療能はさかんになる。諸君は人生の戦いに疲れきったときほど、いっそう多量にこの良薬を用いねばならぬ。

（谷口雅春著『生命の實相』頭注版第7巻より）

Times of sadness are the very moment to laugh and laugh greatly.

Loud and cheerful laughter is the finest tonic that nature has given us. When we burst into laughter our physiological functions that were suppressed by gloominess will be activated immediately. Our circulation will return to normal and our natural healing ability will work vigorously. Friends, to the extent that you are exhausted by the struggles of life, you must take even greater doses of this fine medicine.

From *Seimei no Jissô* (Truth of Life), vol. 7 by Masaharu Taniguchi.

病気は月にかかる雲である 必ず晴れる

　人間の本来は健康なのに、「健康なる実相」の表面に「間違った心」が雲のようにかかって「健康なる実相」をくらまして病気をあらわすのです。病気があらわれるのは、「皎々たる円月」が常にかわらず存在するのに、それに雲がかかって斑点だらけの月があらわれて見えるのと同じことです。
（谷口雅春著『人間そのものの発見とその自覚』より）

Disease is the cloud that covers the moon.
It will surely disappear.

Despite the fact that human beings are originally in perfect health, an *erroneous mind* covers the surface of their *healthy True Image* like a cloud, conceals their *healthy True Image* and gives rise to an illness. The appearance of illness is like the moon that seems blemished by the clouds in spite of the fact that it is always *bright and round.*

From *Ningen Sonomono no Hakken to Sono Jikaku* (The Discovery and Understanding of Human Beings Themselves) by Masaharu Taniguchi.

自己が自由であるためには
他を自由に放ち去れ

　相手を赦すと怪我や病気が治るというだけでなく、それにもまして心が解放される。もし誰かを恨んだり憎んだりしているのならぜひ赦してあげて下さい。恨まれている人より恨んでいる本人の方が苦しいものです。赦すと忽ちスカッとしてスガスガしくなる。相手を祝福してあげる気持になればよいのです。

　　　　　　　（谷口清超著『おんなの幸せ』より）

Release another to gain your own freedom.

Not only does an injury and illness heal when we forgive someone but even much more, our own mind is freed. If you have ill will for or hatred for someone, forgive him in every way. The person who resents another suffers more than the person he resents. When we forgive him we are immediately refreshed and purified. It is best to bless all people.

From *Onna no Shiawase* (The Happiness of Women) by Seicho Taniguchi.

21 他に求める前に自からを変えるがよい

　神は外にあらず。内にまします。生命の自性円満とは即ち仏性であり、神性である。他に求める事をやめよ。他に求める心は争いの因である。真の人格主義は他に求めず、他を奪わず、自己内在の力を礼拝するのである。自分を仏と知って、初めて他の人々をも仏と知るのである。

　　　　　（新選谷口雅春選集11『叡智の斷片』より）

It is best to change yourself before seeking changes in others.

God does not exist outside of us but He resides within. The intrinsic perfection of life is immanent Buddhahood and Divinity. Stop seeking changes in others. The mind that seeks changes is the cause of discord. True individualism does not seek in others or take from them but worships our indwelling power. When we realize that we are the Buddha, for the first time we will know that others are also the Buddha.

From *Eichi no Danpen* (Short Pieces of Wisdom), Shinsen Taniguchi Masaharu Senshû, vol. 11.

人生は自己が主演する舞台である 22

　成功したい者はすでに成功者であるかのように演出し、健康になりたい者はすでに健康であるかのように眉をのばし、役者がある人物を舞台で演ずるように、心から自分のなりたいと思う人物になりきって人生という舞台で演出するとき、その人の「心」は人生でそれを形に現わすにいたるのです。（谷口雅春著『生命の實相』頭注版第2巻より）

Life is a stage and you are its leading actor.

Those who wish to succeed must behave as those they are already successful. Those who seek good health must act as though they are now healthy and cease to frown. When we perform our role on the stage called human life, like an actor on the stage completely identifies with his character, our *mind* will take form in our lives.

From *Seimei no Jissô* (Truth of Life), vol. 2 by Masaharu Taniguchi.

23 全てに感謝せよ
一層よくなるほかはない

　本来悪(あ)しきものはどこにも存在していないのであって、森羅万象ことごとく神の栄光のあらわれんためであります。神の導きを信じ、常に神の心と波長の合った大調和の明るい念を堅持(けんじ)し、感謝しておられましたならば、かならず更に一層よきものがあらわれて来るのであります。
（谷口清超ヒューマン・ブックス１『愛と祈りを実現するには』より）

Let us be grateful to everything. All things can only become better.

In truth evil is nowhere to be found and all things in nature manifest the glory of God. If we always believe in God's guidance, firmly maintain bright thoughts of grand harmony that are in tune with His mind and are grateful to Him, far better things will certainly appear for us all the more.

From *Ai to Inori o Jitsugensuru ni wa* (To Realize Love and Prayer), Taniguchi Seicho Human Books, vol. 1.

病気は「心の影」である
心を変えよ
24

　吾々人間は、「観る通りに顕(あらわ)れる」世界を見て生活しているのであります。如何(いか)に現在の肉体が不健康であるように見えましても、それは単に過去の吾々の「心の影」が今映し出され、業(ごう)が崩れ去って行く状態ですから、それはやがて消え去ってしまうべき運命にあるのであります。
(谷口清超ヒューマン・ブックス1『愛と祈りを実現するには』より)

Disease is a *reflection of the mind.* Let us change our mind.

We human beings are living our lives by watching the *world that appears exactly as we see it.* No matter how unhealthy our physical body may seem to be, it is no more than the reflection of the past *shadow of our mind.* Since our poor health is the state of the collapse and disappearance of karma, it is destined to vanish before long.

From *Ai to Inori o Jitsugensuru ni wa* (To Realize Love and Prayer), Taniguchi Seicho Human Books, vol. 1.

25 与える心になれ 与え返される

　本当に幸せで和やかな生活を送っている人は必ず、与える心、なぐさめ、はげまし、ひとの喜びを共に悦(よろこ)ぶ心をもっています。与える心になり切った時、自分が一番与えられているという結果になる。家庭の中で、よく母が一番愛されているといわれるのは、母が家族に与えて与え尽して来たからである。

　　　　　（谷口清超著『愛する妻と母の話』より）

Acquire the mind of giving and you will be given in return.

Those who are truly happy and live a harmonious life always have a mind of giving that offers solace and encouragement to others and rejoices in the happiness of others. When we completely acquire the mind of giving, we will be given an abundance of everything. The reason why the mother is the most loved member of a family is because she unceasingly gives of herself.

From *Aisuru Tsuma to Haha no Hanashi* (Talks About Darling Wives and Mothers) by Seicho Taniguchi.

26 生命は祖先に始まり子孫につながる

　子供はみな御祖先からのいのちの流れの中で生れて来、大きく育ち、そして又親となり、子を生み育てるということになる。だから当然、御祖先への感謝がなければよく育ちません。家族同士仲よくくらし、ご祖先のお祭りなどもよくして、一家中のいのちが生々と栄えるようにしなくてはならないのです。　（谷口清超著『病いが消える』より）

Our life begins from our ancestors and it is also joined with our posterity.

Children are born, grow up, become parents themselves and give birth to and raise children within the flow of *life* from their ancestors. Therefore it is only natural that they will not grow up well unless we have gratitude to our ancestors. Family members must live in harmony and earnestly memorialize their ancestors so that the *life* of the entire family prospers vibrantly.

From *Yamai ga Kieru* (Illness Vanishes) by Seicho Taniguchi.

27
神の全能のお力が常にささえていて下さる

　ただスラスラと生命の動きのままに活動する時その人の生命は最も伸びやすいのです。仕事をする上に、自分を受けささえてくれる大道(だいどう)は「神」であります。神の全能力がわたしを導き、わたしを受けささえていてくれるから失敗しないと、晏如(あんじょ)として仕事に従事するとき、その人の仕事は伸びるのです。

　　　　（谷口雅春著『生命の實相』頭注版第5巻より）

God's omnipotent power constantly sustains us.

Our life makes progress most easily when we simply take action according to the workings of life itself. When performing our work, the Great Path that is sustaining us is *God*. When we engage in our work with the peace of mind that there is no failure because God's omnipotent power guides and sustains us, our work will make progress and advance.

From *Seimei no Jissô* (Truth of Life), vol. 5 by Masaharu Taniguchi.

28 倒れるということも前進である

　吾人(ごじん)の価値は、幾度(いくたび)も倒れながら再び起き上がり、そのために多くを学び魂を磨き、鍛えて来たことである。諸君の仕事は倒れた体験から多くを学び、一層多くみずから改善するであろう。倒れたままで失敗するのでは値打ちがない。倒れた瞬間にすぐ起き上がって光明に面することである。

　　　　　（新選谷口雅春選集11『叡智の斷片』より）

Even a so called collapse is a step forward.

Our value lies in the many lessons and the polishing and cultivation of our soul from rising to our feet again after stumbling any number of times. You will probably learn much from and make far greater improvements in your work from your failures. There is no value in allowing failure to remain a failure. At the moment of failure we immediately rise to our feet and face the light.

From *Eichi no Danpen* (Short Pieces of Wisdom), Shinsen Taniguchi Masharu Senshû, vol. 11.

良い言葉は相手を生かし自分を生かす

　自分の言葉のアクセントに気をつけましょう。自分の言葉のひびきが周囲の人たちに色々の反応を起させているのです。言葉は創造主(つくりぬし)でありますから柔く温かい感じのする言葉を使うように心掛けていると、次第に自分自身に温かく柔い性格が養成され、容貌までにもあらわれて来るのです。

　　　（谷口雅春著『新版　女性の幸福365章』より）

Good words enliven others and also ourself.

Let us be careful about the tone of our words. Their vibrations cause various reactions in the people around us. Since Word is the Creator, if we strive to use words with a gentle and warm quality about them we will gradually develop a similar character that is manifest even in our features.

From *Shinpan Josei no Kôfuku 365 Shô* (365 Keys to Women's Happiness, new ed.) by Masaharu Taniguchi.

人生は讃嘆のための学校である 30

　どんな人にも優れた所があり、その人でなければならない長所があります。それを見て、言葉で称讃すると、ますます良い所が沢山現われてきて、今までの欠点が消え去って行くのです。それは恰度(ちょうど)月にかかっていたむら雲が、次第に晴れわたり、やがて月が皎々(こうこう)と輝き出すようなものです。

　　　　　　　（谷口清超著『おんなの幸せ』より）

Human life is the school for praise.

Everyone has good points. There are good things that only that person can do. When we recognize those qualities and praise them, an even greater number of good things will appear in him and the faults that plagued him until now will vanish. That is like the clouds over the moon gradually vanishing and revealing the brilliant moon before long.

From *Onna no Shiawase* (Happiness of Women) by Seicho Taniguchi.

31
八方塞がりの時も神様の方向が開いている

　たとい一方の途が塞っていようとも、何も心配することはない。また別の途が開いているのである。たとい八方ふさがりで、あらゆる方角の途が塞がれていようとも、神の子には行き詰りということは無いのである。仰いで高き蒼空を見よ。そこにはあなたの実相の宝座があり、天使たちがあなたを招く。　　　　　（谷口雅春著『生命の讃歌』より）

Even when every path is blocked the way to God is open.

Although a path may be blocked you need not worry. A different path is open for you. Even if everything goes against you and all paths are blocked, there is never a dead end for a child of God. Look up and see the blue sky! In that sky is the jeweled seat of your True Image and the heavenly beings that await you.

From *Seimei no Sanka* (Songs in Praise of Life) by Masaharu Taniguchi.

1989

★

ひかりの言葉
WORDS OF LIGHT

「今」あなたは新生する　1

　神は、「今」新生するとき、過去をもって責め給うことはないのである。神が「今」を吾々に与え給うたことを、神に対して感謝しようではありませんか？「今」は一切の過去を変貌させる力をもっているのである。過去の一切の悪も業(ごう)も罪も、闇と同じような仮(かり)存在に過ぎないのである。

　　　（谷口雅春著『新版　生活の智慧365章』より）

At this *very moment* you are born anew.

When God gives new life to the *present moment* He does not blame us for our past. Shouldn't we be grateful to Him for giving us this moment called *now*? The moment called *now* possesses the power to change our entire past. All evil, karma and sin are nothing but the same temporary existence as darkness.

From *Shinpan Seikatsu no Chie 365 Shô* (365 Keys to Daily Wisdom, new ed.) by Masaharu Taniguchi.

2 日々よきことを必ず実践せよ

　観念の世界から「行(ぎょう)」の世界に超入することが大切である。日々ただ「実行」である。有難いと思うのではなくして、有難いと言うのである。他人(ひと)の喜ぶことを、どんな小さな事でもよいから、実行するのだ。先ず喜びを与えることである。やがて自分の中に沸々(ふつふつ)たる喜びが湧く。
　　　（谷口清超新書文集2『神は生きている』より）

Let's always do good deeds everyday.

It is essential to transcend and enter the world of *practice* from the world of ideas. We must simply *carry out* our ideas every day. We must not only *feel* grateful but *express* our gratitude in words. We must carry out even the smallest acts that bring happiness to others. Above everything else it is essential to give happiness to others. In due course happiness will well up from within you.

From *Kami wa Ikiteiru* (God Is Alive), Taniguchi Seicho Shinshobunshû, vol. 2.

3 愛は限りなく行きとどく

　愛は人間を冷然とふりすてて行くことではないのである、彼を癒して行くことである。大聖者の生涯である。愛深きまなざしは、凡ての生命を生かすのである。愛が行きとどいているのである。そこには今直_{ただ}ちに力一杯の生命が出し切られるのである。「努力なき努力」が流れ出るのである。
（谷口清超ヒューマン・ブックス１『愛と祈りを実現するには』より）

Love is boundless thoughtfulness and care.

Love does not coldly abandon others but heals them. It is the lifetime of a great saint. A deeply loving countenance gives life to all living things. Love is being practiced thoroughly. At that very moment we give of our almighty life completely, and *effortless effort* flows from us.

From *Ai to Inori o Jitsugensuru ni wa* (To Realize Love and Prayer), Taniguchi Seicho Human Books, vol. 1.

「当り前」くらい すばらしいことはない

　あまりにもふんだんに与えられていると、その恩恵に気がつかないことがある。日本の水は豊かで良質だから、平素あまりその有難さに気がつかないが、この恩恵たるや莫大である。父母の愛も、ゆたかで、あふれるばかりだが、その恩恵に気づいていない人々が、如何(いか)に多くいることか。

　　　　　（谷口清超著『輝く日々のために』より）

There is nothing more wonderful than the *ordinary*.

If we always give excessively, people will not feel a debt of gratitude. People are not usually grateful to the water in Japan because of its abundance and good quality. Nonetheless, its blessings are enormous. The love of our parents is abundant and overflowing yet how great are the number of those who are not aware of that blessing.

From *Kagayaku Hibi no Tame ni* (For a Shining Daily Life) by Seicho Taniguchi.

平素の準備が大切である 5

　小さい豆粒のような水の滴でも、常に絶えず少しずつ進撃したら、固い固い岩に孔をあけることができるのです。「常に絶えず少しずつ」の力は、「一気にやって、後はのらくら」よりも大きな進歩をするものです。常に少しずつ進歩するということほど、尊いことはないのです。

　　　　　　　　　（谷口雅春著『人生読本』より）

Constant preparation is important.

Even tiny constant drops of water can bore a hole in a hard rock. *Constant small efforts* achieve greater progress than a sudden great effort that is followed by *idleness*. There is nothing more precious than constant and small progress.

From *Jinsei Dokuhon* (Life's Reader) by Masaharu Taniguchi.

汝の仕事を最高のものとなせ

　人が何かよい物を作り出そうとするならば、そこに・い・の・ち・をかけなければならない。まごころをそそぎ込むのだ。真心のこもった仕事は、愛がなくてはできない。仕事を愛し、人を愛し、国を愛しているとき、なすことに真心がこもるのである。こうして愛の結晶としての傑作が生まれる。

　　　　（谷口清超著『人は天窓から入る』より）

Change your work into a masterpiece.

People must stake their *life* upon a task if they seek to create something good. They must pour in heart and soul. Work that is filled with heart and soul cannot be done without love. When you live by loving your work, your fellow human beings and your country, everything you do will be filled with heart and soul. In this way masterpieces that are the embodiment of love will be born.

From *Hito wa Tenmado Kara Hairu* (We Enter From Heaven's Window) by Seicho Taniguchi.

7 本当に信ずる者はハイを実行する

　本当の信仰には必ず「行動」がともなわなければならないのである。「思い込む」だけであれば、何もしなくてもよい。例えば、夫が"神の子"ですばらしい人だと信ずるということは、妻としての本分を尽し、夫の言葉を神の言葉と信じてハイ（相手と一つになる）を実行することである。

　　　　　　（谷口清超著『妻として母として』より）

Those who truly believe will practice saying "yes."

True faith must be accompanied by *action*. If we simply *make up our mind* we need not make any special effort. For example, in the case of a wife, to believe that her husband is a *child of God* and a wonderful person is to *perform her duty* as a wife, believe that her husband's words are the words of God and practice saying "yes" to him (to be spiritually one with her husband).

From *Tsuma Toshite Haha Toshite* (As a Wife and Mother) by Seicho Taniguchi.

幸福は無限、尽きる事がない

　真の幸福は実の世界にある。実相界は無限である。無限の中にある本体はこれもまた無限である他あり得ないのである。それ故、現実にあらわれる幸福も無限にその質と量とを高揚する。現象界は影の世界であるから、無限の幸福が、吾々の信ずる通りの影を映すのである。
（谷口清超ヒューマン・ブックス１『愛と祈りを実現するには』より）

Happiness is infinite. It can never be exhausted.

True happiness is in the Real World. The True-Image World is infinite. The entity within the infinite can be nothing else than infinite. Therefore the happiness that appears in the actualities infinitely heightens its quality and quantity. Since the phenomena world is a shadow world, infinite happiness reflects the exact shadow that we conceive in our mind.

From *Ai to Inori o Jitsugensuru ni wa* (To Realize Love and Prayer), Taniguchi Seicho Human Books, vol. 1.

子供は神が育て給う

9

　母親がどんなに心配したとて、手でもって子供の心臓を動かしてやることはできないのです。これを動かすのは神様です。では授乳時間のほかはすべてを神に打ちまかせて、家の仕事を、自分の仕事を、良人(おっと)の仕事をズンズンかたづけるがよいのです。そこから教養の時間ができてきます。

　　　（谷口雅春著『生命の實相』頭注版第29巻より）

Children are raised by God.

No matter how mothers worry, they cannot make their child's heart beat with their own hands. It is God who makes the heart beat. Accordingly, except when nursing it is best that they entrust everything to God and steadily attend to their housework, their own tasks and their husband's work. By so doing they will have time to enrich their education.

From *Seimei no Jissô* (Truth of Life), vol. 29 by Masaharu Taniguchi.

徹底して実相を拝め *10*

　少しもよくならないなどと絶望して、実相を拝む行事を中止したらいけないのである。自壊作用が起りつつあるのは、治りつつある転換期だからである。聖書には「終りまで耐え忍ぶものは救われん」と示されているのである。信仰には持続が必要である。忍耐の中に信仰が鍛えられるのである。
　　　　　　　　　（谷口雅春著『女は愛の太陽だ』より）

Thoroughly worship the True Image.

It is wrong to lose hope because of a lack of improvement and to cease to engage in the practices to worship the True Image. This is because the disintegration of the symptoms is the turning point for healing. The Bible teaches that those who endure to the last are saved. Faith requires perseverance. It is within perseverance that faith is forged.

From *Onna wa Ai no Taiyô Da* (Women Are the Loving Sun) by Masaharu Taniguchi.

「道」は近きにあり *11*

　今日(こんにち)の仕事をなし、今日の誘惑を退けよ。人生価値は大きな事業や業績の中にあるのではない。そのうちにも含まれてはいるけれども、日常生活中の瑣(さ)細(さい)な行為の中に、小さないたわりや、思いやりのある微笑や、深切なそこはかとなき行為の中にある。瑣細なことの中にその人の真の愛があらわれる。

　　　　（谷口雅春著『新版　女性の幸福365章』より）

The *Way* is near at hand.

Do today's work and avoid the day's temptations. The value of human life is not in large enterprises or achievements. While there is also value in such things, it is in the small deeds in daily life, the little *kindnesses*, a warm smile and a considerate *artless* deed that value exists. Within his small deeds a person's true love manifests.

From *Shinpan Josei no Kôfuku 365 Shô* (365 Keys to Women's Happiness, new ed.) by Masaharu Taniguchi.

他の人の幸福を喜ぶ心が仏心である

　他の喜びに対して同喜することは、常に誰でも必ずしも出来ることではないのである。真の愛は、他(ひと)の喜びを見て、自分も亦(また)喜べなければならないのである。他の出世を見て、わが子の出世のように喜び、他の成功を見て、わが子の成功のように思える者であってこそ「真に愛する」ものである。
（新選谷口雅春法話集7『生活と人間の再建』より）

The mind that rejoices in the happiness of others is the Buddha-mind.

We are not always able to rejoice in the happiness of others. True love must feel happy when seeing that others are happy. When others are promoted think of it as our own child's promotion and rejoice. And when seeing that others have succeeded, feel that our own child has become a success. Those who can think such thoughts are indeed *truly loving* people.

From *Seikatsu to Ningen no Saiken* (Rebuilding of Daily Life and Human Beings), Shinsen Taniguchi Masaharu Hôwashû, vol. 7.

「愛」の完成は「神への全托」である

「愛」は、「尽す」こと自体に悦(よろこ)びを見出す。「愛」は実行である。いと小さな愛行が、地に埋(う)もれる時、それはいつしか多くの種子を結ぶ。しかしその時が、何時(いつ)になるかを知ろうとするな。「愛」の完成は、「神への全托」の繰り返しによって、初めて実現されるのである。

（谷口清超著『人は天窓から入る』より）

The consummation of *love* is *complete trust in God.*

Love discovers joy in the act of *making effort* itself. *Love* is practice. The smallest loving deed that is planted in the earth will someday produce much good seed. Yet you must not seek to know when that good seed will appear. The consummation of *love* is realized for the first time by constant *complete trust in God.*

From *Hito wa Tenmado Kara Hairu* (We Enter From Heaven's Window) by Seicho Taniguchi.

信じ切る者は癒される 14

　見せかけの「苦難」にとらえられて「もう駄目だ」と絶望をせず、ただひたすらに「神の子・人間」を信じ、感謝と祈りと愛との生活に徹せられたならば、必ずよくなって行くのである。常に私達を愛し、みまもり給うところの無限絶対の「神様」を想い観ることが何よりも大切なのである。

　　　　　　　　　（谷口清超著『感謝の奇蹟』より）

Those who thoroughly believe will be healed.

Do not be a captive of make-believe *sufferings, feel discouraged* and lose hope. Simply believe intently in the *child of God human-being*, and thoroughly live a life of gratitude, prayer and love. By so doing you will surely improve. To meditate on and visualize the infinite and absolute *God* who always loves and protects us is more important than anything else.

From *Kansha no Kiseki* (The Miracles of Gratitude) by Seicho Taniguchi.

受けたりと信じて明るく行動せよ 15

　祈りは、「受けたりと信じて、その如く行動せよ」ということですから、もう祈りが実現したつもりになって、そのように"実演する"とよいのです。ある学校へ入りたければ、その学校の写真をながめて、毎日そこへ通っている自分を「祈る」などと、具体的に、行動的に祈るのがよい。

　　　　　　　（谷口清超著『あなたは伸びる』より）

Believe that you have already received and cheerfully take action.

Prayer is to *believe and take action as though you have already received.* Therefore it is best to believe that your prayer is already realized and act out your belief. If you wish to enter a certain school, look at its picture and *pray* that you are daily attending classes there. Such concrete and active *prayers* are effective.

From *Anata wa Nobiru* (You Will Grow) by Seicho Taniguchi.

16 よろこびと感動をもって仕事をなせ

　画家は描くことに悦(よろこ)びを感ずるから描くのだ。音楽家が音楽を奏でるのも、弾くことが悦びだから弾奏する。人生は総合的な表現芸術であるから、この人生を創作し発表し表現するのはまさに「悦ぶため」である。何もしないでいるとかえって苦痛となる。何でも力一杯、よろこんでやらなくてはならない。(谷口清超著『輝く日々のために』より)

Engage in your work with joy and inspiration.

An artist paints because he feels joy in his work. A musician performs his music because the act of playing is a joy for him. Since human life is an all-embracing expressive art, it is exactly for the *sake of joy* that we create, present and express our work of life. To sit and do nothing becomes a source of pain. We must do everything happily and with might and main.

From *Kagayaku Hibi no Tame ni* (For a Shining Daily Life) by Seicho Taniguchi.

17 来るものは拒むな、悦んで受けよ

　すべてのものは、それを素直に受けて味わうとき屹度何らかの獲得となる。これが天地一切のものと和解する道である。それらが損失と見えるのは、自分がある立場に執して、ある立場からのみそれを観るからである。人生のあらゆる経験に於て"絶対損失"になるものは一つもないのである。

（谷口雅春著『新版　栄える生活365章』より）

Do not reject what comes but accept it with joy.

There is surely something to be gained when we honestly and obediently accept all things and appreciate them. This is the way to reconcile oneself with everything in the universe. Things appear to be a loss because we are attached to a certain fixed viewpoint and base all our judgments on it. In every experience of human life there is not a single *total loss*.

From *Shinpan Sakaeru Seikatsu 365 Shô* (365 Keys to a Prosperous Life, new ed.) by Masaharu Taniguchi.

愛によって敵も味方となる 18

　人を冒(おか)す心が自分に残っていると、相手から自分を冒す物が現れて来る。何者にも冒されないようにしようと思ったら、天地一切のものと和解しなければならないのです。自分自身が変ることによってのみ敵が変るのです。イエスが「汝の敵を愛せよ」といったのは、そのことなのです。

　　　　　（谷口雅春著作集第3巻『女性の本質』より）

Through love even an enemy becomes a friend.

When we have thoughts of harming others things that bring harm will appear around us. If we wish to be free of harm we must be reconciled with all things in the universe. It is only by changing ourselves that our enemy will change into a friend. This is why Jesus taught that we must love our enemies.

From *Josei no Honshitsu* (Essence of Women), Taniguchi Masaharu Chosakushû, vol. 3.

19 「待つ」時間は決して無駄ではない

「持続し耐えしのぶ」ということも一つの「力」である。この能力をあらわすには、どうしてもある程度の"漸進(ぜんしん)"が必要なのである。それは一種のよろこびである。それはあたかも"婚約時代"の如き甘美さを秘めている。その香(か)わしき匂いを知らせるために、人々は待つことを命ぜられる。

（谷口清超著『さわやかに生きよう』より）

The time spent *waiting* is by no means fruitless.

To *wait and endure* is also a kind of *strength*. To manifest this ability requires a certain *gradual progress*, which is a sort of happiness that conceals a sweetness like the period of engagement. In order to know that fragrance, we have been ordered to wait.

From *Sawayakani Ikiyô* (Let's Live a Refreshing Life) by Seicho Taniguchi.

我に無限の勇気あり 20

　勇気を欲する者は、既に、「自分には勇気がある」と念ずるがよい。毎日々々「自分は神の子であるから勇気がある、勇敢である」と念ずるがよい。その実行が繰返されるとき潜在意識に「我に勇気あり」の暗示が度重なって印象され、本当に、勇気ある実相があらわれて来ることになる。

　　　（谷口雅春著『新版　生活の智慧365章』より）

There is infinite courage within me.

Those who seek courage should think "I am already courageous." They should daily think, "Since I am a child of God, I am courageous and brave." By repeating this practice the suggestion "I am courageous" is impressed on our subsconsciousness and our courageous True Image indeed appears.

From *Shinpan Seikatsu no Chie 365 Shô* (365 Keys to Daily Wisdom, new ed.) by Masaharu Taniguchi.

21 自己弁解をすて、理想に生きよ

　人間は仏子であり神の子でありますから完全な自由を有するのです。それ故、誰にも責任を負わせない何事にも全責任を自分に負う強い心に立ち帰り、いっさいの口実を捨て、いっさいの自己弁解を捨て、ただ驀らに自分の理想とするところに進んで行けばよいのであります。

　　　　（谷口雅春著『生命の實相』頭注版第23巻より）

Throw away self-justification and live your ideal.

Since human beings are children of Buddha and children of God, they possess perfect freedom. That is why it is best that we recover our powerful mind that blames no one but accepts responsibility for everything, discard all excuses and self-justification and simply advance at full speed toward our goal.

From *Seimei no Jissô* (Truth of Life), vol. 23 by Masaharu Taniguchi.

今からでも遅くない、全力を出せ 22

　今からでも遅くない。神は時間を超越していたまうから、今からでも神の方へ振向けば、いつでも神の祝福を受けることができるのである。私たちは心が神に振向いた瞬間から自己改善がはじまるのである。祈りを深めることによって普遍の神に波長を合わすがよい。

（谷口雅春著『新版　女性の幸福365章』より）

It is not too late.
Do your very best.

It is not too late. Since God transcends time, if we turn to God from this very moment we can receive His blessings at any time. From the moment that our mind turns to God our self-improvement begins. We should tune our wavelengths to the Universal God by deepening our prayer.

From *Shinpan Josei no Kôfuku 365 Shô* (365 Keys to Women's Happiness, new ed.) by Masaharu Taniguchi.

惜しみなく愛の言葉を与えよ 23

　日本の男性の多くは、とかく無口であり、妻に対する愛情の表現を極力ひかえ目にする傾向があるが、言葉というものは行為の源泉であり、身・口・意の三業が種子となって、果を生ずるのである。従って、愛や思いやりの言葉を惜しみなく与えることも、それ相当の豊かな果を収穫する秘訣である。　　　　（谷口清超著『日本よ永遠であれ』より）

Generously give words of love.

Many Japanese men are reluctant to talk and rarely express their love for their wife. However, word is the source of action and the seed of the three karmas of body, mouth and mind, and gives rise to results. Therefore to generously give words of love and understanding is the secret to receive similar abundance in return.

From *Nippon Yo Eien de Are* (O Japan, May You Be Eternal) by Seicho Taniguchi.

24 如何(いか)なる時も神の御胸(みむね)に抱(いだ)かれている

　私たちの周囲の万物はすべて私たちを祝福し、祝福の讃歌を歌ってくれていることを、私たちは魂の耳をもって聞くことができるのである。私たちは、神に祝福され、神に愛され、神の愛に囲繞(とりま)かれ護(まも)られているのである。何時(いつ)如何なる時にも神の護りから外れるということはないのである。

　　　　　（谷口雅春著『聖経版　真理の吟唱』より）

At all times you are in God's embrace.

With the ears of our soul we can hear all things in our surroundings blessing us and singing their songs of praise. We are blessed by God, loved by Him and surrounded and protected by His Love. At any moment we are never outside of His embrace.

From *Seikyôban Shinri no Ginshô* (Meditations on Truth, sutra edition) by Masaharu Taniguchi.

よき心こそ富の中の富である

「豊かな心」とは、あれが足らぬ、これが不足していると思う心ではなく、ここにこんなすばらしいものがある、あそこにもとてもいい人がいると、「足りている世の中」を見る心のことである。今迄見すごしていた「豊かなかくれた富」へ、心の眼を振り向けることである。

（谷口清超著『さわやかに生きよう』より）

A cheerful disposition is indeed the essence of wealth.

An *abundant mind* is not the mind that thinks of want and insufficiency but the mind that sees the *world of sufficiency* where there are *such* wonderful things and good people. It is to turn our mind's eye to the *hidden abundant wealth* that we had overlooked until now.

From *Sawayakani Ikiyô* (Let's Live a Refreshing Life) by Seicho Taniguchi.

善行は必ず善果をもたらす 26

　きゅうりになすが実るということはないのだ。この因果律は人間の精神生活にも通用し、行為の善悪によって、その結果の善悪が決まるのである。善行（ぜんこう）が善果を生み、悪行（あくぎょう）が悪果をもたらす。その時期は未定であり、一般には予測され難い。けれども善行は必ずいつかは善果を生むものである。

　　　　　　　（谷口清超著『困難に戯れよう』より）

Good deeds will surely bring good results.

An *eggplant* will never grow from a *cucumber plant*. This law of cause and effect also applies to the mental life of human beings. The good or bad of our actions determines the good or bad of the results. Good deeds produce good results and evil deeds bring evil results. The time for the results to appear is undecided and it is generally difficult to predict. Yet good deeds will surely produce good results someday.

From *Konnan ni Tawamureyô* (Let's Play With Difficulties) by Seicho Taniguchi.

27 愛は表現しなければならぬ

　愛は表現しなければなりません。「表現されたる最(いと)と小さき愛も、表現されざる偉大なる愛にまさる」と云(い)う諺があります。「愛」はこれを表現したときに本当に相手を幸福にし、その相手の幸福にあふれる表情を見、言葉をきき、雰囲気を感じて、あなた自身が一層幸福になれるのです。

　　　　　（新選谷口雅春選集10『新女性讀本』より）

Love must be expressed.

Love must be expressed. There is a saying that even the smallest love that is expressed is superior to a great but unspoken love. When *love* is expressed it truly brings happiness to others, and we ourselves become far more happy when we see their countenances that are overflowing with happiness, hear their words and feel their happy atmosphere.

From *Shin Josei Dokuhon* (New Reader for Women), Shinsen Taniguchi Masaharu Senshû, vol. 10.

私心を棄てた時、神があらわれる 28

　神の導きを受けるには、私心を去らなければならないのである。湯呑みに一杯すでに湯が入っているところへ、どんな美味しいお茶を注いでも、みな流れ出てしまう。どんな立派な神のお導きのアイディアでも、私心で一杯になっている"心の湯呑"の中には入らないのである。

（谷口雅春著『国のいのち　人のいのち』より）

When you throw away selfishness God appears.

To receive God's guidance we must discard selfishness. No matter how much delicious tea we pour into a teacup already full with hot water, the tea will trickle away. And no matter how excellent the ideas of God's guidance that we receive, they will not enter our *mind's teacup* that is filled with selfishness.

From *Kuni no Inochi Hito no Inochi* (The Life of a Nation and the Life of Its People) by Masaharu Taniguchi.

29 吾れ祈れば天地応え、吾れ動けば宇宙動く

　あなたが"神の子"であるということを自覚すれば、何処へ往こうとも其処が"神の国"であり、極楽浄土である。"神の子"たるいのちの頂点に立つとき、南極の中心のポイントに立てばどの方向を向いても北であると同じように、どの方向を向いても神と偕にあるのである。

（谷口雅春著『生命の讃歌』より）

When I pray the universe responds.
When I move the universe moves.

When you realize that you are a *child of God*, no matter where you go that place is the *Kingdom of God* and the Pure Land of Utmost Bliss. When you stand on the peak of *life* that is the *child of God*, in the same way that you are always facing the North when at the center of the South Pole, no matter where you turn you are always one with God.

From *Seimei no Sanka* (Songs in Praise of Life) by Masaharu Taniguchi.

神に祈れ、道は必ず開かれる 30

　吾々は神の子として、すべての善きものは与えられているのである。信じて祈って、「既にそれは与えられております。有りがとうございます」と感謝するとき、放送局のスタジオで実演されていることがテレビのブラウン管面にあらわれて来るように、あなたの運命としてあらわれて来るのである。（谷口雅春著『新版　生活の智慧365章』より）

Pray to God.
The way will surely open.

As children of God we are given all good things. "I have already been given what I seek. Thank you very much." When we believe and pray in this way and offer our gratitude, just as the performance in the television studio appears on our television picture tube, our prayer will take form as our destiny.

From *Shinpan Seikatsu no Chie 365 Shô* (365 Keys to Life's Wisdom, new ed.) by Masaharu Taniguchi.

仕事を通して神の愛を伝えよ

31

　今日から毎日一回人に喜ばれることをせよ。どんな小さいことでもよい。紙屑(かみくず)を拾うことでもよい。それを実行すれば、必ず生き甲斐(がい)が出て、喜びが湧く。なぜなら人間は「神の子」であり、神の愛に充(み)ち溢(あふ)れ、人を愛し、いたわり、役立ちたいという思いに満たされているからである。

　　　　　（谷口清超著『輝く日々のために』より）

Convey God's Love through your work.

From today let us bring happiness to someone once a day. Even the smallest deed is fine. You could even pick up scraps of paper. By practicing such deeds you will surely feel the worth of living and joy will well up from your soul. Why? Human beings are *children of God* and filled to overflowing with His Love and brimming with the desire to love others, to be kind and considerate, and to be of service.

From *Kagayaku Hibi no Tame ni* (For a Shining Daily Life) by Seicho Taniguchi.

参考図書

谷口雅春著　聖経版 続 真理の吟唱
谷口雅春著　青年の書
谷口雅春著　生命の實相　頭注版第14巻
谷口清超著　病いが消える
谷口雅春著作集第5巻　人間無病の原理
谷口清超著　さわやかに生きよう*
谷口清超著　父と母のために
谷口雅春著　新版 栄える生活365章
谷口清超著　人は天窓から入る*
谷口清超著　輝く日々のために*
谷口清超ヒューマン・ブックス9　善意の世界
谷口雅春著　若人のための78章*
谷口雅春著　新版 女性の幸福365章
谷口清超新書文集2　神は生きている
谷口雅春著　新版 ひかりの語録
谷口清超著　輝く人生のために*
谷口雅春著　新版 生活の智慧365章
谷口清超ヒューマン・ブックス1　愛と祈りを実現するには
新選谷口雅春選集11　叡智の斷片*
谷口雅春著　生命の實相　頭注版第2巻
谷口清超著　栄える人々のために*
谷口雅春著　生命の實相　頭注版第5巻
谷口清超著　家庭をたのしく
谷口雅春著　新版 希望を叶える365章
谷口雅春著　人間そのものの発見とその自覚
谷口雅春著　生命の實相　頭注版第7巻
谷口清超著　おんなの幸せ*
谷口清超著　愛する妻と母の話*
谷口雅春著　生命の讃歌
谷口雅春著　人生読本
谷口清超著　妻として母として*
谷口雅春著　生命の實相　頭注版第29巻
谷口雅春著　女は愛の太陽だ
新選谷口雅春法話集7　生活と人間の再建
谷口清超著　感謝の奇蹟
谷口清超著　あなたは伸びる*
谷口雅春著作集第3巻　女性の本質
谷口雅春著　生命の實相　頭注版第23巻
谷口清超著　日本よ永遠であれ*
谷口雅春著　聖経版 真理の吟唱
谷口清超著　困難に戯れよう*
新選谷口雅春選集10　新女性讀本*
谷口雅春著　国のいのち　人のいのち*

＊は品切れ中
上記図書はすべて日本教文社刊

References

Taniguchi Masaharu. *Seikyôban Zoku Shinri no Ginshô* (Meditations on Truth II, sutra edition).
——. *Seinen no Sho* (For Young People).
——. *Seimei no Jissô* (Truth of Life), vol. 14.
Taniguchi Seicho. *Yamai ga Kieru* (Illness Vanishes).
Taniguchi Masaharu. *Ningen Mubyô no Genri* (Principle of Perfect Health for Human Beings), Taniguchi Masaharu Chosakushû, vol. 5.
Taniguchi Seicho. *Sawayakani Ikiyô* (Let's Live a Refreshing Life).
——. *Chichi to Haha no Tame ni* (For Fathers and Mothers).
Taniguchi Masaharu. *Shinpan Sakaeru Seikatsu 365 Shô* (365 Keys to a Prosperous Life, new ed.).
——. *Hito wa Tenmado Kara Hairu* (We Enter From Heaven's Window).*
——. *Kagayaku Hibi no Tame ni* (For a Shining Daily Life).*
——. *Zen-i no Sekai* (World of Good Intentions), Taniguchi Seicho Human Books, vol. 9.
Taniguchi Masaharu. *Wakôdo no Tame no 78 Shô* (Seventy-Eight Lessons for Young People).*
——. *Shinpan Josei no Kôfuku 365 Shô* (365 Keys to Women's Happiness, new ed.).
Taniguchi Seicho. *Kami wa Ikiteiru* (God Is Alive), Taniguchi Seicho Shinshobunshû, vol. 2.
Taniguchi Masaharu. *Shinpan Hikari no Goroku* (Sayings of Light, new ed.).
Taniguchi Seicho. *Kagayaku Jinsei no Tame ni* (For a Shining Human Life).
Taniguchi Masaharu. *Shinpan Seikatsu no Chie 365 Shô* (365 Keys to Daily Wisdom, new ed.).
Taniguchi Seicho. *Ai to Inori o Jitsugensuru ni wa* (To Realize Love and Prayer), Taniguchi Seicho Human Books, vol. 1.
Taniguchi Masaharu. *Eichi no Danpen* (Short Pieces of Wisdom), Shinsen Taniguchi Masaharu Senshû, vol. 11.*
——. *Seimei no Jissô* (Truth of Life), vol. 2.
Taniguchi Seicho. *Sakaeru Hitobito no Tame ni* (For Prosperous People).*
Taniguchi Masaharu. *Seimei no Jissô* (Truth of Life), vol. 5.
Taniguchi Seicho. *Katei o Tanoshiku* (A Happy Home Life).
Taniguchi Masaharu. *Shinpan Kibô o Kanaeru 365 Shô* (365 Keys to Realize Your Hopes, new ed.).
——. *Ningen Sonomono no Hakken to Sono Jikaku* (The Discovery and Understanding of Human Beings Themselves).
——. *Seimei no Jissô* (Truth of Life), vol. 7.
Taniguchi Seicho. *Onna no Shiawase* (The Happiness of Women).*
——. *Aisuru Tsuma to Haha no Hanashi* (Talks About Darling Wives and Mothers).*
Taniguchi Masaharu. *Seimei no Sanka* (Songs in Praise of Life).
——. *Jinsei Dokuhon* (Life's Reader).
Taniguchi Seicho. *Tsuma Toshite Haha Toshite* (As a Wife and Mother).*
Taniguchi Masaharu. *Seimei no Jissô* (Truth of Life), vol. 29.
——. *Onna wa Ai no Taiyô Da* (Women Are the Loving Sun).
——. *Seikatsu to Ningen no Saiken* (Rebuilding of Daily Life and Human Beings), Shinsen Taniguchi Masaharu Hôwashû, vol. 7.*
Taniguchi Seicho. *Kansha no Kiseki* (The Miracles of Gratitude).
——. *Anata wa Nobiru* (You Will Grow).*
Taniguchi Masaharu. *Josei no Honshitsu* (Essence of Women), Taniguchi Masaharu Chosakushû, vol. 3.
——. *Seimei no Jissô* (Truth of Life), vol. 23.
Taniguchi Seicho. *Nippon Yo Eien de Are* (O Japan, May You Be Eternal).*
Taniguchi Masaharu. *Seikyôban Shinri no Ginshô* (Meditations on Truth, sutra edition).
Taniguchi Seicho. *Konnan ni Tawamureyô* (Let's Play With Difficulties).*
Taniguchi Masaharu. *Shin Josei Dokuhon* (New Reader for Women), Shinsen Taniguchi Masaharu Senshû, vol. 10.*
——. *Kuni no Inochi Hito no Inochi* (The Life of a Nation and the Life of Its People).*

---

* Currently not in print.
Above books are published by Nippon Kyobunsha Co. Ltd.

人生の扉を開く―日英対訳で読む　ひかりの言葉―

2005年 7 月 5 日　初版発行
2020年 9 月10日　6 版発行

監修者………谷口清超　〈検印省略〉©Seicho-No-Ie, 2005

発行者………西尾慎也

発行所………株式会社日本教文社
　　　　　　東京都港区赤坂9―6―44　〒107―8674
　　　　　　電話　03（3401）9111（代表）
　　　　　　　　　03（3401）9114（編集）
　　　　　　FAX　03（3401）9118（編集）
　　　　　　　　　03（3401）9139（営業）
　　　　　　https://www.kyobunsha.co.jp/

頒布所………財団法人世界聖典普及協会
　　　　　　東京都港区赤坂9―6―33　〒107―8691
　　　　　　電話　03（3403）1501（代表）
　　　　　　振替　00110―7―120549

印刷…………東港出版印刷株式会社
製本…………牧製本印刷株式会社

カバー挿画…鯰江　光二

◆…………乱丁本・落丁本はお取り替えいたします。
◆…………定価はカバーに表示してあり　ます。

ISBN978-4-531-05248-6　Printed in Japan